The Militia of 1569 AD

Introduction

In the England of 1569, the traditional enemy was France; but if France was hated, thanks to "Bloody Mary", Spain was detested.

When a new Spanish ambassador arrived in London, he was refused residence in the Palace of Whitehall, and ignored. As a result of the anti-Spanish feeling in the country the ambassador suggested to Philip of Spain that England could only be dealt with "sword in hand".

Elizabeth's government was also reaching the same conclusion about Spain.

Militia Mobilisation

Two Acts of Parliament laid down the regulations for the calling out of the militia.

There was a scale of arms and armour, each eligible male was expected to provide his share, under pain of a two pound fine, or ten days imprisonment.

The demands were substantial; all men between the ages of 16 and 60 who qualified (all but the very poorest) were to attend. This was not so they could be trained, but to ensure that they had the required equipment. The muster would be announced in the local parish church and the "petty" constable was supposed to jog the memories of those who preferred to forget their obligations.

The muster was as much a social occasion as a military one. They were held at traditional times, Easter, Whitsun, and Michaelmas. It was much more of a parade than an inspection.

The Weaponry

Unless everyone was required to parade simultaneously items tended to be lent from village to village, this defeated the whole point of the Acts.

Privately owned arms and armour were a sign of a man of substance, but many parishes held common armouries. This explains the many references to weapons held "jointly". Perhaps some of these armouries were unwittingly donated by the Spaniards themselves.

"I will confess here, that by trickery I have drawn 2000 corselets from the royal arsenal at Malines [The Spanish Netherlands - present day Holland] *and they are now in England. You will understand that their disappearance has created no small stir amongst the [Spanish] officers"*

Sir William Cecil

Training

These militiamen were ordered to march in their armour, with weapons, for up to six miles, under penalty of four days in prison. Although initially complaining, with regular musters [and surely these men would have been fitter than we today, for lack of mechanised transport] these men who "would have given good sums of money to have been exempted from the service," as a constable said, "rejoice in that they have profited by the training."

The Gunpowder Revolution

The Militia, being England's first line of defence in the event of an invasion, were caught up in controversy over the decline of the English longbow, and the increasing use of muskets. The English found it difficult to accept that the age of the cloth-yard shaft was over, as this contemporary shows us.

"[The foreigners] turn up their tailes and cry 'shoot English' ... the breech of such a varlet should have been nailed to his bum with one arrow and another feathered in his bowels before he should have turned about to see who shot the first"

The militia were themselves not eager to be reequipped because of the increased expense, a bullet was gone forever, an arrow could be reused.

However, their initial fears overcome, the troops began to enjoy shooting practice. From about 1570 the bow had had its day. In the future, two of the four day musters were to be spent "principally in the shot with the bullet."

Further reading

Norman Longmate "Defending the Island"

Alexander McKee "From Merciless Invaders"

David A. Thomas "The Illustrated Armada Handbook"

Duff Hart-Davis "Armada"

Peter Padfield "Armada"

Paul Kennedy "The Rise and Fall of the Great Powers"

A.J.Howard and T.L.Stoate "The Devon Muster Roll for 1569"

Glossary of Terms

Almen Rivet

A form of armour consisting of a bulbous breastplate with a laminated skirt defense called tassets, simple, round shoulder and forearm guards held together by leather straps and sliding rivets for a wide range of motion.

Caliver

A forerunner of the rifle and other longarm firearms. It was an improved version of the arquebus or Harquebuse. The caliver, was introduced in the early 16th century. The word is derived from the English corruption of calibre, or the size/width of the barrel.

Harquebuse

An early form of musket. See front cover.

Gelding

A horse

Gorgette

Armour covering the neck

Militia

The 'Dad's Army' of the day, roughly equivalent to our Territorial Army.

Pike and Bill

A long shafted spear with variously shaped blades, particularly effective against cavalry

Presenters Sworen

The influential men of the village or area, who were sworn to present an accurate assessment of the arms of the militia.

Splints

Armour for the arms.

Steel Cap

A helmet

The Militia Attendance List 1569 AD

Devon / Coleridge Hundred / Aishebrenton Parrishe

William Pearse

Nicholas Hilhaye

John Edmond

William Perret

Who do presente as aforesaide [Some of those below brought extra weaponry and armour]

Presenters sworen

William Somaster Esq 2 corselet, 2 Calivers instead of 1 2

Thomas Drewe Esq Steel caps and 2 bills

Thomas Lakington

William Pears 2 Gorgetts

Margaret Ellet 1 pair splints

The inhabitants not particlarlie chardged by the statute are acessed to fynde one corslet, 4 calivers, 20 pikes

The names of all the habell menne within the sayde parishe of Aishebrenton mustered

Archers

Gregory Dottyn

Henry Shorte

Thomas Jones

Richard House

John Lorye

John Hilley

Richard Forde

Roger Bennet

Robert Sherpham

John Kowle

Tibalde Skotte

Harquebusiers

Lewes Davye

Robert Rewe

John Sharpham

Henry Jones

Anthony Browne

John Hawkinge

Pikemen

Henry Lye

Nicholas Lye

Roger Ferries

Thomas Sullocke

William Pears

George Nycoll

Billmen

Thomas Tude

John Bunker

John Edmonde

John Lye

Jarveys Bennet

William Stoyle

Simon Babyn

William Martyn

John Jones

William Lye

Robert Steven

Anthony Adam

Richard Lorye

John Burges

Henry Ryder

Devon / Coleridge Hundred / Portlemouth Parrishe

Presenters sworen

John Neale

Alexander Chrispyn

John Wakeham

Ellice Lamb

Who do presente as afforsaid

John Neale

Alexander Chrispyn

Richard Wakeham

John Pope

William Ponde

The inhabitants not particlarlie chardged by the statute of armour and weapons are acessed 2 calivers, tenne pikes

The names of all thabell menne within the saide parishe of Portlemouth mustered

Archers

Alexander Crispyn

John Wakeham

Walter Wakeham

Harquebusiers

John Neale

Richard Tollye

Pikemen

Peter Putte

William Lye

Billmen

John Stone

Ellice Lamball

Thomas Walter

William Stone

William Goodyer

John Jackeman

John Pynwell

Roger Putte

Andrew Lowringe

Peter Putte

William Willinge

Devon / Coleridge Hundred / Chivelston Parrishe

Presenters sworen

John Marche

Thomas Came

John Perett

John Wadlonde

Who do presente as afforsaide

John Porte

John Marche

Thomas Kame

John Wadlond

William Sowllock

Robert Partridge

William Shotte

The inhabitants not particlarlie chardged by the statute are acessed to fynde 2 Calivers, tenne pikes

Archers

Thomas Denys

John Wadlond

John Sullocke

Harquebusiers

Roger Gillarde

Pikemen

William Collynge

Richard Stone

John Marche

William Meade

John Phillip

John Ellyce

William Foster

John Watts

John Forde

Christopher Wolcombe

Richard Steven

William Porte

Richard Steven

William Porte

Thomas Partridge

William Haradon

Philip Shootman

John Hardye

Walter Stone

John Walter

Roger Wakeham

John Esvache

Robert Balle

William Shoote

Richard Abraham

Billmen

Robert Collyn

Thomas Collyn

John Tabbe

James Letson

Roger Partridge

William Choppe

William Hynne

Walter Tome

Robert Putte

John Earell

William Walter

Robert Partridge

John Tome

Richard Browse

William Sullocke

John Pownde

Devon / Stanborough Hundred / Thorleston Parrishe

Presenters sworen

Thomas Stephen

Walter Harrye

Thomas Comishe

Andrew Roger

Who do presente as afforesaid

Thomas Stephens without a steel cap

The inhabitants not particlarlie chardged by the statute are acessed to fynde 4 Calivers

The names of all the habell menne within the saide parishe of Thorleston mustered

Pikemen

Thomas Stephens jnr

Robert Squyre

John Shepherd

John Squyre

William Comishe jnr

Thomas Comishe

Thomas Rider

Robert Marrodd

Andrew Roger

Robert Comishe

John Harrye

John Randell

John Harward

Ralph Toker

Billmen

Thomas Stephens sen

Robert Toker

Ralph Yeoman

John Yeoman

Richard Birdwood

John Wille

Humphrey Stere

John Drewe

Andrew Phillip

Stephen Blackaler

William Home

Roger Bevill

John Balle

Devon / Ermington Hundred / Ugborough Parrishe

Presenters sworen

Richard Fawell

William Founteyn

Thomas Cawnterell

Nicholas Cole

Humphrey Clotworthye

John Revell

Who do present as aforsaide

William Edwards gent

William Fownteyn

William Trenick 1 jack and splints, 1 bow, 1 sheaf of arrows, 1 steel cap

John Glasse 1 Almen Rivets, 2 bows, 2 sheafs of arrows

Robert Bonde

Richard Lappe without a steel cap

John Androwe 1 Jack and splints, 1 bow, 1 sheaf of arrows, 2 steel caps, 1 bill

William Stidston 1 Almen Rivet, 1 bill

Richard Brokinge 1 Jack and splints, 1 steel cap, 1 bill

John Chubbe 1 Jack, 2 bows, 2 sheafs of arrows, 1 steel cap, 1 bill

John Revell 1 Jack, 1 bow, 1 sheaf of arrows

John Lappe

The inhabitants not particularlie chardged by the statute of armour

are acessed to fynde 12 Calivers, 20 pikes

The names of all thabell menne within the sayde parishe of Ugborough mustered

Archers

Thomas Jeffry

John Borne

Lewes Wood

Adam Ulcomb

Edward Hayman

John Byrte

William Trenycke

Henry Hayman

Thomas Fox

Nicholas Towpe

Harquebusiers

William Symons

Hugh Hatche

William Guynes

Richard Myrthe Sen

John Baron

John Lange

Robert Lappe

Pascoll Drake

Robert Wythe

Arthur Toser

Michael Steven

Humphrey Claworthy

Richard Fursman

Mathew Tumor

Thomas Conney

Steven Revell

Pikemen

John Revill

John Fox

Richard Bourne

John Towpe

John Reynolds

John Androwe

Thomas Comishe

William Bury

Richard Conney

Robert Foster

James Stidson

Andrew Hille

John Landall

Richard Shoote

Robert Bonde

Billmen

Thomas Androwe

Robert Towpe

Philip Lighe

Richard Michelmor

William Damarell

Stephen Showtman

Thomas Toser

John Mudge

Adam Blackall

Robert Mighell

John Baker

William Standinge

Richard Cood

Simon Hargest

Henry Hatche

Devon / Ermington Hundred / Modbury Parrishe

Presenters sworen

Oliver Hille Esq

Thomas Prediaux Esq

William Fortescue Esq

John Androwe

John Harte gent

John Edgecombe

Who do present as aforesaide

Henry Champernown Esq 2 light geldings furnished, 2 Corslets, 2 Almen Rivets, 2 pikes, 2 bows, 2 sheafs of arrows, 2 brigandynes, 1 harquebuise, 1 murrain

Thomas Prediaux Esq 1 light gelding

Oliver Hille Esq 1 light gelding

William Fortescue 1 light gelding

John Harte gent 1 light gelding, 1 corslet, 1 pike

John Rowse 1 corslet, 2 almen rivets, 2 pikes

Henry Wens ton 1 bow, 1 sheaf of arrows

Osmond Frinde 1 bow, 1 sheaf of arrows, 1 bill

George Frinde 1 bow, 1 sheaf of arrows, 1 bill

Richard Fostard 1 bow, 1 sheaf of arrows, 1 bill

William Shepperd

Henry Gille

Humphrey Damerell 1 bow, 1 sheaf of arrows

William Willinge 1 bow, 1 sheaf of arrows, 1 bill

John Starre 1 almen rivet and splints, 1 bow, 1 sheaf of arrows, 1 bill

John Edgecombe 1 bow, 1 sheaf of arrows, 1 bill

John Wakeham 1 bow, 1 sheaf of arrows, 1 bill

John Weringe

Richard Crappyn

John Swete 1 almen rivet, 1 bow, 1 sheaf of arrows

John Frinde of Stokingbridge 1 almen rivet, 1 steel cap, 1 bill

Wilmot Baker widow 1 Corslet, 1 bill, 1 murr

Robert Shepperd 1 almen rivet, 1 bill

John Wancot without 1 bill

Philip Osborne without 1 bill

Christopher Shepperd 1 bow, 1 sheaf of arrows, 1 bill, 1 steel cap

Peter Murche 1 Harquebuise, 1 murr, 1 bill

William Odymer 1 pair of brigandynes, 1 bow, 1 sheaf of

Peter Murche 1 Harquebuise, 1 murr, 1 bill

William Odymer 1 pair of brigandynes, 1 bow, 1 sheaf of arrows, 1 steel cap

Peter Shepperd

Vincent Whitinge and Otes Oldrive 1 almen rivet, 1 steel cap 1 bill each

The inhabitants not particlarlie chardged by ye statute are acessed to fynde and maynteyn at their comune charge 2 corslets, 40 pikes, 10 calivers

The names of all hable menne within the said parishe of Modburye mustered

Archers

John Androwe John Will ins John Wyncott

John Edgecombe Henry Fourde

John Castell

Richard Vennynge

Osmund Fourde

John Preiste

James Lapthome

John Pollyblanke

George Fourde

Anthony Shenner

Richard Facye

Humphrey Damerell

Thomas Collyford

Richard Crappen

John Anneys

Harquebusiers

John Frynde

Robert Frinde

Richard Canamor

John Yeallinge

Richard Efforde

Simon Listen

Peter Hille

James Jones

John Wakeham

Andrew Walter

Thomas Bright

Thomas Fourde

William Hayre

John Cole

Jerome Thome

Arthur Dever

Robert Holman

Hugh Martyn

Robert Crosse

Robert Lyant

Nicholas Odemir

Ellice Crocker

Thomas Stenelake

Thomas Morshed

Otes Oldryve

Thomas Hingeston

John Willinge

Peter Marche

William Ryder

Pikemen

Nicholas Forde

Gregory Lampe

Richard Clynche

William Willinge

Nicholas Marche

William Derent

John Steven

Christopher Shepperd

Thomas Gorye

Henry Dever

John Crossman

John Lome

Thomas Falenger

Richard Quyler

William Baker

Thomas Yeoman

John Adam

John Willinge

Robert Brokinge

Billmen

William Shepherd

Christopher Elliot

John Loper

John Swete Henry

John Myles

John Heyman

Wynston Henry Morrys

John Chapell

John Gye

William Fourd

John Whiddon

Nicholas Chappell

Roger Warde

John Lyan

Thomas Weryn

Robert Dever

Thomas Willinge

Thomas Foster

Nicholas Warde

William Soper

John Weryn senior

Walter Foster

Robert Shepperd

John Weryn junior

Henry Gyll

Thomas Hille

John Frinde

Robert Howse

Edward Crappen

James Cawker

John Cole

John Wakeham

John Worthe

Thomas Goulde

John Gille

John Hooper

Robert Hastinge

Nicholas Hingeston

Richard Boyes

John Potell

Hugh Hellyer

Richard Foster

William Shirwill

Devon / Ermington Hundred / Awton Gifford Parrishe

Presenters sworen

Anthony Honeychrche

Richard Costerd

John Sture

William Coyte senior

Who do presente as afforesaid

Anthony Honeychurche Esq 1 Corslet, 2 bows, 2 sheafs of arrows 2 Harquebuises

Hugh Harrye 1 almen rivet, 2 bows, 2 sheafs of arrows, 1 caliver

Richard Costerd

John Cole

John Saverey

William Coute 1 Harquebuise, 1 steel cap, 1 bill

Anthony Phillip

Hugh Home

John Treste 1 almen rivet, 1 bow, 1 sheaf of arrows

John Wakeham

Henry Tabbe

Richard Sherif 1 pair of splints

John Shurif 1 pair of splints

William Waringe

Robert Seyward 1 pair of splints

John Shirriefs

John Phillip

Roger Gaye

Simon Coyte

James Gibbe 1 almen rivet, 1 bow, 1 sheaf of arrows

The inhabitants not particlarlie chardged by the statute are acessed to fynde and have tenne calivers, 20 pikes

The names of all the habell menne within the saide parishe of Awton Gifforde mustered

Archers

George Hatche

Richard Showte

Hugh Balle

Thomas Flesheman

Richard Horswill

William Werryn

Harquebusiers

John Heurchurche

Richard Snowdon

Hugh Lighe

Richard Phillipp

John Bowryn

Christopher Clarke

Pikeman

John Morrys

Richard Shirrief

John Hayes

George Shirrief

Edward Hingeston

John Shirrief

John Snowdon

John Bowman

Ambrose Ellyot

William Lee

Henry Tabbe

Anthony Cleif

William Shynner

John Campe

John Wakeham junior

John Shirrief

Richard Wakeham

James Choppe

Richard Elwarde

Thomas Coxer

William Wolston

Billmen

John Tabbe John

Harrys Richard

Cole William

Harryes Jerome

Hayes John

Wakeham

Robert Wakeham

Robert Snowdon

Robert Towson
Simon Mighell
Roger Gaye
Jeffry Wakham
William Coyte
Thomas Coyte
John Kellye
Robert Collyn
George Ellet
William Tabbe
Anthony Phillips
Robert Shepperd
John Comishe
John Horswill
John Payne
John James
William Snowdon
Henry Hinxton
William Balle
Robert Cleif
Stephen Cole
Edward Snowdon
Robert Stower

Devon / Ermington Hundred / Herfforde Parrishe / Herfforde Parrishe

Presenters sworen

Henry Mason

John Scobill

Who do presente as aforesaide

Richard Williams

Henry Mason

John Boyes

John Bawyn

The inhabitants not particlarley chardged by the statute are acessed to fynde 1 corslet, 2 calivers

The names of all the habell menne within the saide parishe of Herfforde mustered

Archers

Philip Fynche

John Ryder

William Horsman

Harquebusiers

Robert Person

William Fourde

Pikemen

Robert Williams

Christopher Willinge

Billmen

Henry Mason

John Boyes

Adam Flood

Thomas Pedill

Christopher Holman

Thomas Hingeston

Robert Fourde

Adam Hanaforde

John Boyes

Devon / Ermington Hundred / Kingeston Parrishe

Presenters sworen

Robert Aisheforde

William Shepperde

William Roger

Who do presente as aforesaid

Robert Aisheforde gent 1 corselet, 2 calivers

William Shepherd 1 corselet, 1 bill

John Warde 1 almen rivet, 1 bill

Thomas Williams}

Nicholas Palmer}

Robert Palmer}

Thomas Hatche} 1 almen rivet, 1 bow, 1 sheaf of arrows, 1 bill jointly

Philip Lyssyn 1 pair of splints, 1 steel cap, 1 bill

Walter Aisheford}

John Michelmor}

Richard Warde} 1 almen rivet, 1 bow, 1 sheaf of arrows, 1 bill jointly

William Warde}

William Snedall}

William Roger}

Robert Warde} 1 almen rivet, and splints, 1 bow, 1 sheaf of arrows, 1 steel cap, 1 bill jointly

Nicholas Walle}

Thomas Hardwaye}

John Towson}

Andrew Veale} 1 almen rivet, 1 bow, 1 sheaf of arrows,

William Eastligh} 1 bill jointly

Thomas Harvye of Lanxton 1 almen rivet, and splints, 1 steel cap, 1 bill

Edward Cawker 1 pair splints, 1 steel cap, 1 bill

The inhabitants not particularlie chardged by ye statute are acessed to fynde etc 2 calivers, tenne pikes

The names of all the habell menne within the sayde parishe of Kingeston mustered

Archers

William Shepperd

Harquebusiers

Walter Aisheford

Nicholas Palmer

Nicholas Malborowe

Anthony Canamor

John Harrys

Thomas Stone

John Michelmor

Richard Baron

Thomas Willinge

Pikemen

William Roger

John Towson

Andrew Veale

Robert Palmer

William Yaebbesley

Thomas Shepperd

Billmen

John Warde

John Lovell

John Shepperd

John Webber

Nicholas Palmer

Robert Warde

Nicholas Evelinge

Chris. Cheseman

Nicholas Walker

Robert Balle

Thomas Cawse

Richard Warde

John Belle

John Coffyn

William Warde

Philip Blacke

John Cooke

John Toker

Peter Shepperd

Richard Saunder

Robert Sterte

John Leache

Nicholas Shepperd

William Lowde

Devon / Ermington Hundred / Holberton Parrishe

Presenters sworen

John Heale

Walter Chubbe

Richard Came

Who do presente as aforesaid

Andrew Hillersdon Esq 1 corselet, 2 Almen rivets, 1 pike, 1 bow, 1 sheaf of arrows, 1 steel cap, 1 bill

Thomas Burell gent 1 light gelding furnished, 2 calivers

Walter Strecheley gent 1 light gelding, 1 caliver

John Heale 1 corselet, 1 pike, 1 bow, 1 sheaf of arrows, 1 bill, 1 caliver

Walter Chubbe 1 almen rivet and gorgett, 1 steel cap, 1 bill

John Chubbe 1 almen rivet, 1 harquebuse, 1 steel cap

The following have each 1 almen rivet, 1 stele cap, 1 bill

Richard Came

John Avente

Margaret Burell

John Drake

John Potell

John Crispyn

John Gittisham

John Beale

Walter Dollyn

Walter Woode

John Hingeston

The Inhabitants not particularlie chardged by the statute are acessed to fynde 4 calivers, 30 pikes

The names of all the habell menne within the saide parishe of Holberton mustered

Archers

John Clerke

Bartholomew Bond

Nicholas Collyn

Harquebusiers

Walter Strecheley

John Lake

John Horwill

Richard Trevill

Richard Hinxton

David Elliott

Thomas Veale

John Crispyn

William Pottell

Thomas Came

Thomas Marshall

George Perye

Thomas Harys

Richard Stockman

John Veale

Andrew Trevy

Adam Crocker

Edward Veale

John Wythe

Alexander Holman

John Bartlet

Thomas Renoll

John Pridiaux

Richard Harte

Pikemen

Walter Wood

Adam Stevens

Andrew Cotley

John Cauker

Thomas Pears

Vincent Roper

Roger Hinxton

John Ley

John Ley[no mistake]

Robert Awton

John Walke

Henry Cryspyn

Roger Knighte

Ralph Hinxton

John Steven

Thomas Ley

Billmen

John Heale

William Tirrell

Ellice Trevye

John Broke

John Davy

Richard Weighte

John Lake

Richard Norris

Andrew Foster

Thomas Pomery

John White

John Dottyn

John Madoke

John Robbyns

John Midelton

Andrew Ley

Peter Renoll

Ellice Facye

John Harte

Andrew Elliot

John Chubbe

William Veale

Bartholomew Cauker

William Cotlighe

John Crispyn

Robert Walke

Walter Eveling

John Catlegh

Walter Ley

John Holman

Walter Woodmor

William Skryche

John Shepperd

David Frye

Peter Madocke

Andrew Hinxton

John Salman

William Paule

Henry Crispyn

Adam Crispyn

Devon / Ermington Hundred / Ermington Parrishe

Presenters sworen

Edward Streicheley gent

John Bonvile

John Spelte

Thomas Brokinge

Who do presente as aforesaid

John Bondvile Esq 1 light gelding, 2 corselets, 1 pike, 1 bow, 1 sheaf of arrows, 1 steel cap, 1 bill, 2 calivers 1 murrain

John Spalte 2 calivers, 1 murrain

Following five have 1 caliver

Thomas Cleif

Thomas Brokinge

Henry Lagasike

Thomas Edgecomb

Henry Edgecomb

Richard Howsdon 1 bow, 1 sheaf of arrows, 1 steel cap, splints

John Pridiaux 1 almen rivet, 1 bill

The inhabitants not particularlie chardged by the statute are acessed to fynde etc 3 calivers, 20 pikes

The names of all thabell menne within the sayde parishe of Ermington mustered

Archers

John Bonvile

Richard Platyn

John Barret

Thomas Edgecomb

John Tom

William Toker

William Lawde

Thomas Maye

John Lavors

Thomas Wood

Philip Moysse

John Spalte

John Allyn

John Brokinge

Henry Edgecombe

Richard Collyn

Thomas Sawnder

Richard Riche

Hugh Rowe

Thomas Allyn

George Roper

Roger Cole

Harquebusiers

Richard Coule

James Mighell

Pikemen

William Mason

Stephen Lapthome

William Mighell

Richard Ripley

Christopher Riche

John Roche

Henry Reche

John Ripley

Thomas Aishe

Robert Langman

Walter Northe

William White

Richard Brodmead

Richard Chubbe

Richard Benet

Henry Lagasike

John Willinge

Henry Lagasike

Henry Hinxton

William Purcomb

Billmen

Thomas Cleif

John Chaple

John Dustayn

Richard Mighell

John Cleif

John Honeywill

John Fox

William Cleif

Christopher Lye

Henry More

Thomas Lagasike

John Hodge

Richard Franklyn

Francis Chapell

Richard Chubbe

William Weymoth

Thomas Broking

George More

George Cropp

Christopher Fox

Thomas Cleif

John Pears

John Perott

Thomas Lavors

Walter Spurwell

John Browne

Walter Wolcomb

Richard Pedle

John Whitefilde

Thomas Luppyncott

Devon / Ermington Hundred / Rydmoure Parrishe

Presenters sworen

John Norreis

Robert Frowde

Who do presente as aforesaid

John Norries 1 almen rivet

Robert Froode 1 pair of splints, 1 steel cap, 1 bill

Thomas Yeolland 1 almen rivet, 1 pair of splints, 1 steel cap, lbill

The following nine share between them 2 almen rivets, 2 bows, 2 sheaf of arrows

Robert Cawker

Roger Cawker

Nicholas Ellet

William Hatche

Blanche Ellet

Richard hatche

Thomas Palmer

Joan Geyn

Robert Tabbe

William Rowe and James Ebbesleghe 1 almen rivet between them

The inhabitants not particularlie chardged by the statute are acessed to fynde and have 1 corselet, 2 calivers

The names of all thabell menne within the saide parishe of Rydmor mustered

Archers

William Browne

Richard Browne

Pikemen

William Rawe

Philip Palmer

William Treworthye

Robert Foude

William Cole

Nicholas Cawker

John Hache

Nicholas Yeolland

John Lewes

Billmen

James Yeabsley

Thomas Edmonds

Richard Godfrey

Francis Stabbe

John Palmer

William Why

William Hatche

John Sollocke

ten Robert

William Gaye Tabbe

Devon / Ermington Hundred / Bigburye Parrishe

Presenters sworen

John Strobridge gent

William Burley gent

John Marwood

Who do presente as aforesaid

Thomas Pearse 1 bow, 1 sheaf of arrows, 1 pair of splints

The inhabitants not particularlie chardged by the statute are acessed to fynde and have 2 corslets, 2 calivers

The names of all thabell menne within the saide parishe of Bigburye mustered

Archers

John Strobridge

Richard Riche

John Cooke

Hugh Willinge

Harquebusiers

John Turpyn

John Baldwyn

Thomas Mooringe

Stephen Parnell

William Plishe

Richard Paige

Simon Coyte

Richard Parnell

Walter Cooke

John Jolle

William Webber

William Nosse

Hugh Wakeham

Pikemen

George Towson

John Jane

John Giles

John Bytte

Billmen

John Marrowd

Richard Kitte

John Hache

John Randell

Thomas Pears

John Wakeham

Robert Harwood

John Bowdon

John Coyte

Hugh Norrys

John Webber

William Thome

William Randell

John Forde

Richard Harte

William Shoote

John Ellyott

Thomas Home

Henry Plishe

www.ingramcontent.com/pod-product-compliance
Ingram Content Group UK Ltd.
Pitfield, Milton Keynes, MK11 3LW, UK
UKHW020217250726
13967UKWH00001B/53